The Slave Dancer

by Paula Fox

Reproducibles

and Teacher Guide

Senior Editor: Marsha James
Editor: Terry Ofner
Permissions
Coordinator: Cynthia M. Martin
Art Director: Randy Messer
Cover Photo: The Granger Collection

Reviewers: **Lula Armstead**
                      Crenshaw, Mississippi

                      Margaret Drew
                      Hyde Park, Massachusetts

                      Sarah Smith Ducksworth
                      Union, New Jersey

                      Robert Gish
                      San Luis Obispo, California

Acknowledgment
Book Builders Incorporated
Research, Design, Production

TABLE OF CONTENTS

About the Novel

About Africa

About the Middle Passage

About American Slavery

continued

TABLE OF CONTENTS

continued

Comparative Works

Suggested Activities

Acknowledgments

From *The New York Times Book Review*. Copyright © 1974 by The New York Times Company. Reprinted by permission.

From *The Slave Dancer* by Paula Fox. Copyright © 1973 by Paula Fox. Reprinted with the permission of Bradbury Press, an affiliate of Macmillan, Inc.

From *The Slaves* by Susanne Everett. Copyright © 1978 by Bison Books.

From *The Transatlantic Slave Trade* by James A. Rawley. Copyright © 1981 by James A. Rawley. Published by W. W. Norton & Company, Inc.

From *Africa Remembered*, "Four Nineteenth Century Nigerians." Copyright © 1961 by the Regents of the University of Wisconsin. Published by the University of Wisconsin Press.

From *A Slaver's Log Book* by Captain Theophilus Conneau. Copyright © 1976 by Howard S. Mott, Inc. Published by Prentice-Hall, Inc.

From *To Be a Slave* by Julius Lester. Copyright © 1968 by Julius Lester. Published by Dial Press.

From *A Pictorial History of the Slave Trade* by Isabelle Aguet, translated by Bonnie Christen. Copyright © 1971 by Editions Minerva, S. A., Geneve. Published by Minerva Books Ltd.

From *Black Voyage*, edited by Thomas Howard. Copyright © 1971 by Thomas Howard. Published by Little, Brown & Company.

From *Eyewitness to History*, edited by John Carey. Copyright © 1987 by John Carey. Published by Harvard University Press.

From *Slavery*, edited by William Dudley. Copyright © 1992 by Greenhaven Press. By permission of the publisher.

From *Classic Slave Narratives*, edited and with an Introduction by Henry Louis Gates, Jr. Copyright © 1987 by Henry Louis Gates, Jr. Published by New American Library.

From *Puttin' on Ole Massa*, edited by Gilbert Osofsky. Copyright © 1969 by Gilbert Osofsky. Published by Harper & Row, Publishers.

From *Roots* by Alex Haley. Copyright © 1976 by Alex Haley. Published by Doubleday & Company. By permission of the publisher.

From *My Name Is Not Angelica* by Scott O'Dell. Copyright © 1989 by Scott O'Dell. Published by Houghton Mifflin Company.

From *The Women of Plums* by Dolores Kendrick. Copyright © 1989 by Dolores Kendrick. Published by William Morrow and Company, Inc.

From *Generations* by Lucille Clifton. Copyright © 1976 by Lucille Clifton. Published by Random House.

TEACHER INFORMATION

Welcome to *Latitudes*

Latitudes is designed for teachers who would like to broaden the scope of their literature and history study. By providing fascinating primary source documents and background information, the *Latitudes* collection of reproducibles helps your students link a fiction or nonfiction book with its historical framework.

The series broadens students' understanding in other ways too. Each packet offers insights into the book as a piece of literature, including its creation, critical reception, and links to similar literature.

The *Latitudes* selections help readers draw on and seek out knowledge from a unique range of sources and perspectives. These sources encourage students to make personal connections to history and literature, integrating information with their own knowledge and background. This learning experience will take students far beyond the boundaries of a single text into the rich latitudes of literature and social studies.

Purposes of This Packet

The material in this *Latitudes* packet for *The Slave Dancer* has been carefully chosen for four main purposes.

1. to help students connect contemporary and historical events
2. to encourage students to pose questions about the effects of slavery on the individual and society
3. to provide resources that help students evaluate what's "real" in *The Slave Dancer*
4. to help students use the skills and content of both social studies and language arts to search for meaning in the novel

Contents of This Packet

The reproducibles in this packet have been organized into six sections.

- About the Novel
- About Africa
- About the Middle Passage
- About American Slavery
- Comparative Works
- Suggested Activities

About the Novel

The resources here introduce students to contextual dimensions of the novel. Selections include

- a plot synopsis
- biography of Paula Fox
- critics' comments about *The Slave Dancer*
- key excerpts from *The Slave Dancer*
- a glossary of historical and technical terms from the novel and from resources in the *Latitudes* packet
- a timeline of the history of slavery in the United States
- a map of the triangular trade
- a visual of New Orleans

About Africa

These reproducibles familiarize students with the experiences of Africans both before and after their enslavement. Selections include

- two remembrances of life in Africa
- first-person accounts by the captain of a slave ship and a ship's surgeon

About the Middle Passage

These reproducibles provide first-person accounts of life aboard a slave ship from several different perspectives. Selections include

- accounts of the Middle Passage by an enslaved African, a sailor, and an English slave trader turned abolitionist
- first-person accounts of a slave revolt, a scene in which slaves were forced to dance, and a shipboard epidemic

About American Slavery

These reproducibles introduce students to the experiences of enslaved Africans after they arrived in the Americas. This section includes

- first-person accounts by a witness of a slave auction, an enslaved person, and Frederick Douglass
- contrasting viewpoints on slavery

Comparative Works

In this section, selections give students a literary dimension to their study. The reproducibles offer

- excerpts from theme-related novels
- a theme-related poem, a memoir, and songs
- a suggested reading and viewing list

Suggested Activities

Each reproducible in the packet is supported with suggestions for student-centered and open-ended student activities. You can choose from activities that develop reading, writing, thinking, speaking, and listening skills. Projects are suitable for independent, collaborative, or group study.

Use of the Material

The pieces in *Latitudes* can be incorporated into your curriculum in any order you wish. We encourage you to select those resources that are most meaningful and relevant to your students.

Story Synopsis

The year is 1840. Thirteen-year-old Jessie Bollier lives in New Orleans with his mother and his younger sister. The Bollier family has been very poor ever since Jessie's father drowned in a steamboat accident. In order to earn a few extra pennies, Jessie sometimes visits the waterfront and plays his fife for the sailors.

One night, as he returns home from an errand, Jessie is kidnapped by two men. The men carry him to their ship, *The Moonlight*. "We're going to take you on a fine sea voyage," says one of the sailors. Jessie is shocked to find that he is a prisoner on a slave ship. The ship is sailing to Africa to pick up its human cargo.

Eventually Jessie learns why he was kidnapped. He is to "dance" the slaves. With his fife, he will provide music for the slaves to dance to. Traders believe that the practice keeps the slaves in salable condition during the long sea trip. All Jessie can think of is escaping so he can return to his family.

On the trip to Africa, Jessie begins to learn a little about the captain and crew of *The Moonlight*. Captain Cawthorne is a cruel man, whose only concern is the money he can make through the illegal slave trade. Most of the members of the crew either mock Jessie or ignore him. One exception is Purvis, an Irish sailor who takes Jessie under his wing. Purvis explains the slave trade to Jessie.

Upon reaching Africa, *The Moonlight* waits offshore for its cargo. Jessie is horrified to witness naked men, women, and children brutally shoved onto the ship.

After the captives are crammed together in the dark hold of the ship, *The Moonlight* begins its return voyage. Daily the Africans are brought on deck to "dance" to the music of Jessie's fife. Those who refuse or can't stand up are whipped. When Jessie protests, he is whipped also.

To add to the torment of the return voyage, a deadly fever breaks out among the Africans. This enrages Captain Cawthorne because every sick slave means a loss of money. Furiously, he orders the infected slaves to be thrown overboard in an attempt to control the spread of the disease.

When the ship reaches Cuba, a Spanish slave trader boards *The Moonlight*. Captain Cawthorne stages an elaborate spectacle for the merchant. He forces the Africans to dress in outlandish costumes, and then he breaks open a keg of rum. As they drink, a lookout spies an American ship on the horizon. The ship is coming to enforce the antislavery laws.

continued

Alarmed, Captain Cawthorne orders his crew to throw all the Africans overboard and to outrun the American ship. At the same time, a violent windstorm breaks out.

In the confusion, Jessie manages to escape below deck with an African boy named Ras. The two boys hear the storm raging as they huddle together in the hold. The ship finally breaks apart, and Jessie and Ras are flung into the ocean.

Somehow the boys manage to struggle to the gulf shore of Mississippi. There they meet a fugitive slave named Daniel, who helps them regain their strength.

After Ras rests for a few weeks, Daniel arranges for him to be taken to freedom in the North. Daniel also tells Jessie how to return to New Orleans.

After his homecoming, Jessie works for a while in New Orleans. But he finds that he cannot stand to live in the midst of slavery. So he moves north to Rhode Island. Later he sends for his mother and his sister.

The events of 1840 eventually fade from Jessie's memory. But his months on the slave ship have one lasting effect. Jessie is never able to listen to music again without thinking of the tormented African slaves on board *The Moonlight*.

About the Author

Paula Fox

In accepting the Newbery Medal for *The Slave Dancer* in 1974, Paula Fox explained why she writes. "I write to discover, over and over again, my connection with myself, with others." For many years, Fox's novels have helped readers discover relationships between themselves and others as well.

Fox's novels often feature characters who are forced to live far from home. This is probably a reflection of her own childhood. Fox was born half Spanish and half Irish-English. Her parents were actors who performed all over the country. These travels kept them from providing a stable home. So they sent young Paula to live in New York City with friends—a minister and his ailing mother. The minister was a former newspaper reporter and a wonderful storyteller. His home was filled with books. Inspired by the minister's love of words, Paula became an enthusiastic reader. At five years of age, she announced her intention to become a writer.

But Paula didn't remain with the minister for long. In 1931 when Paula was seven, she left to live with family friends in California. A short time later, she spent two years in Cuba with her grandmother. After that, she moved again. By the time she was twelve, Paula had attended nine schools. She called herself a traveling child who moved every year or two and seldom saw her parents.

Since she was always the "new kid," Paula was shy with other children. So the aspiring writer sought comfort in books. For her, public libraries became "places of refuge amid chaos and confusion."

Changes continued to shape Fox's life. As an adult, her jobs took her to places as far away as England and Poland. Fox was a newspaper reporter for several years. She also worked as a machinist at a steel mill, taught school, and edited movie scripts. Writing remained at the "edges" of her life.

Eventually Fox settled in New York City, married, and began a family. Only after her two sons became young adults did she begin to write books.

In her novels Fox tries to introduce young people to things they have never seen. In *The Slave Dancer,* she wanted to show her readers the distant world of slavery. She felt it was important that young people understand what slavery did to the enslaver as well as to the slave. "There are those who feel that slavery debased the enslaved," Fox explained. "It is not so. Slavery engulfed whole peoples, swallowed up their lives, committed such offenses that in considering them, the heart falters, and the mind recoils. Slavery debases the enslaver."

Fox explored another kind of captivity in her award-winning novel *How Many Miles to Babylon?* This novel, written in 1967, is about the life of a black child in the ghetto. It has been called "one of the first contemporary books for young adults to deal with the harsh realities of life for a black child in the inner city." Two other books of Fox's which have received numerous awards are *One-Eyed Cat* and *The Moon-lit Man.*

Today Paula Fox still lives in New York City, and she continues to write steadily.

Critics' Comments

*When **The Slave Dancer** was first published in 1973, most critics praised the novel. Some, however, deemed it a failure. The following statements reflect both kinds of comments.*

The Slave Dancer is historical fiction at its finest, for Fox has meticulously researched every facet of the slave trade and of the period. . . . The Slave Dancer takes the reader on a voyage that reveals a haunting glimpse into the abyss of human evil. . . . The Slave Dancer is clearly Fox's masterpiece, and it is fast becoming a classic in American children's literature.

—Anita Moss
Dictionary of Literary Biography

. . . each of the sailors is sharply individualized, the inhuman treatment of the captives is conveyed straight to the nose and stomach rather than the bleeding heart, and the scenes in which Jessie is forced to play his fife to "dance the slaves" for their morning exercise become a haunting, focusing image for the whole bizarre undertaking.

—Kirkus Reviews

Jessie is our window on the slave trade and it is here that the novel fails. As a character, Jessie simply is not interesting. He becomes a mere device for the transmission of information about life on a slave ship and the slave trade in Africa and the Americas. The information, however, never takes on a living reality, because we do not care about Jessie. Thus it is difficult to care about what he sees.

Throughout the novel the young hero is passive, accepting his own capture with scarcely a word of protest and even developing a warm affection for Purvis, one of his kidnappers. Jessie's reactions to the slave trade are "correct," i.e. he is horrified and sympathizes with the captured Africans. Exactly why is unclear, because he has grown up in the slave South and the author does not draw the character sharply enough to explain why he is atypical of his culture. We are asked to accept him on faith. I couldn't.

None of the characters, however, are much more than devices. The slave ship captain is a second-rate Wolf Larsen and the crew only a little less villainous. The Africans are depicted as rather pathetic and dumb creatures, so much so in fact that it is difficult to have sympathy for them. Maybe slave ship crews were villainous and African slaves pathetic, but their portrayal as such here simply isn't convincing.

What saves this book from being a failure is the quality of the writing, which is consistently excellent. With such good writing, it is too bad that the book as a whole does not succeed. This novel describes the horrors of the Middle Passage, but it does not re-create them, and if history is to become a reality, the reader must live that history as if it were his own life. In *The Slave Dancer* we are only spectators and we should have been fellow sufferers—as slave traders and slaves.

—Julius Lester
The New York Times Book Review

Voices from the Novel

The following quotes are from ***The Slave Dancer****.**

I heard men's voices. Hands gripped me through the canvas. I was tossed, then trussed[1], then lifted up and carried like a pig to market. (13)

Without a word of warning, the little man snatched me up in his arms, held me fast to his chest and bit my right ear so hard I screamed. (23)

The truth came slowly like a story told by people interrupting each other. I was on a ship engaged in an illegal venture, and Captain Cawthorne was no better than a pirate. (34)

Nicholas Spark flogged Purvis' shirt from his back. Beneath the leaping of the rope, blood and cloth mixed. The sun began to die on the horizon, and still he beat him. (42)

Not all the gabble of the sailors, the sustained flow of the wind that drove us on, could mask the keening of the slaves as they twisted and turned on the water casks, or struggled to find an edge of one of a handful of straw pallets upon which to rest their shackled ankles. I dozed. I woke. Never to silence. (62)

I played on against the wind, the movement of the ship and my own self-disgust, and finally the slaves began to lift their feet, the chains attached to the shackles around their ankles forming an iron dirge, below the trills of my tune. (67)

But except for Stout and Spark and the Captain, the men were not especially cruel save in their shared and unshakable conviction that the least of them was better than any black alive. (72)

I can't think what impulse moved me, but I took the fife from my lips and whispered my name to the boy. Only that. *"Jessie!"* And as I whispered, I pointed at myself. I began to play at once. The boy's eyes never left my face that morning. (74)

In not much more time than it takes to tell it, Nicholas Spark was bound with a rope and pushed to the rail and there dropped over. Just before he disappeared beneath the water, I swear he took three steps. (76)

At that moment, Sam Wick picked up a black woman and simply dropped her over the side. With hardly a pause, he then kicked over two men. (104)

* All page numbers provided are from the Dell Laurel-Leaf Historical Fiction edition of the book.

[1] *trussed*: tied up or bound

GLOSSARY

*Understanding what the following terms mean may be helpful as you read **The Slave Dancer**.*

Andersonville: Confederate prison in Georgia where appalling conditions led to the deaths of 12,000 Union prisoners of war.

Bight of Benin: wide bay in the Gulf of Guinea in western Africa.

boatswain: ship's officer in charge of the deck and its crew.

cabociero: title of a Portuguese trader who negotiated the price of slaves.

carronade: light cannon used at close range.

chandler: maker or seller of candles.

doldrums: ocean regions near the equator noted for dead calms and light breezes; sailing ships often came to a halt in the region because of a lack of wind.

Emancipation Proclamation: document signed by President Abraham Lincoln in 1863 that freed the slaves in the Confederacy.

impress: to force someone to serve in a military group or on board a military ship.

indentured servant: person who agrees to work for another for a specified time.

macaroon: term used for an African considered too old or too sick to work.

Middle Passage: the typical route of slave ships across the Atlantic Ocean from West Africa to the West Indies or the American continent. The term is used to refer to the slave trade.

press gang: military detachment or group that forced individuals to perform military service.

slave revolt: uprising among enslaved persons.

Glossary of Nautical Terms

Understanding what the following sailing terms mean may be helpful as you read ***The Slave Dancer.***

boom: pole extending from a mast to keep the bottom of a sail stretched out.

bow: the front part of a ship.

bowsprit: large, tapered pole extending from the front of a ship to which ropes or cables supporting the masts are attached.

brail: small rope attached to a sail that is used to haul the sail in.

galley: the kitchen of a ship.

halyard: rope for raising or lowering a sail.

hull: the frame or body of a ship.

mast: tall pole rising from the deck of a ship to which the sails are attached.

mizzenmast: the third mast from the front in a ship that contains three or more masts.

ratline: thin piece of tarred rope that serves as part of a ladder for climbing the rigging.

rigging: ropes and other gear used to support and control the masts, yards, and sails.

sheet: rope attached to the lower corner of a sail; used to control the set of the sail.

shroud: rope stretched from a ship's side to a mast to offset the strain on the mast.

skiff: small, light, open boat.

tarpaulin: sheet of waterproof canvas used as protection from water.

yard: slender rod attached at right angles to a mast and used to support a sail.

A Time in HISTORY

The following timeline traces some of the major events that occurred before slavery was abolished in the United States.

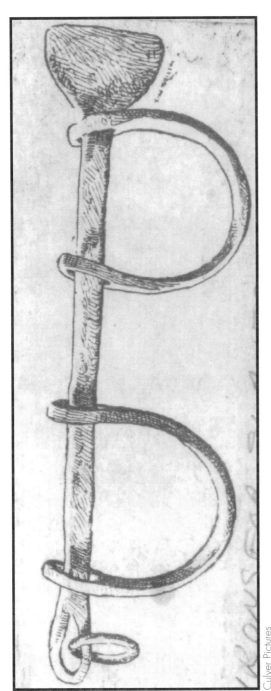

Leg irons

1600

A Dutch ship brings 20 African indentured servants to Jamestown, Virginia (1619)

The *Rainbowe*, the first American slave ship, sails (1645)

1650

First major slave revolt, Gloucester, Virginia (1663)

1700

Slave revolt in New York City; nine settlers killed in street fighting (1712)

Rumor of slave revolt in New York City causes 18 slaves to be hanged, 13 to be burned at the stake, and 70 to be sold to the South (1741)

1750

Vermont becomes the first American state to abolish slavery (1777)

U.S. Constitution allows the continuation of slavery for 20 years (1787)

1800

Great Britain outlaws British slave trade; United States outlaws the importation of Africans for slavery (1807)

1850

Fugitive Slave Law requires all citizens to aid in the return of runaway slaves to masters (1850)

Dred Scott decision; the U.S. Supreme Court denies that slaves have any legal rights (1857)

Clothilde, the last slave ship, arrives in Mobile, Alabama (1859)

Thirteenth Amendment to the Constitution abolishes slavery (1865)

The Geographical Picture

Triangular Trade

One side of the triangle was formed by American ships crossing the Atlantic to Africa with cargoes of rum. The rum was traded for slaves, and it was also served to African traders to make them drunk. The second side of the triangle was formed when these ships sailed from Africa to the West Indies to sell the enslaved Africans and buy molasses. The triangle was completed when the molasses was brought to New England to be made into more rum.

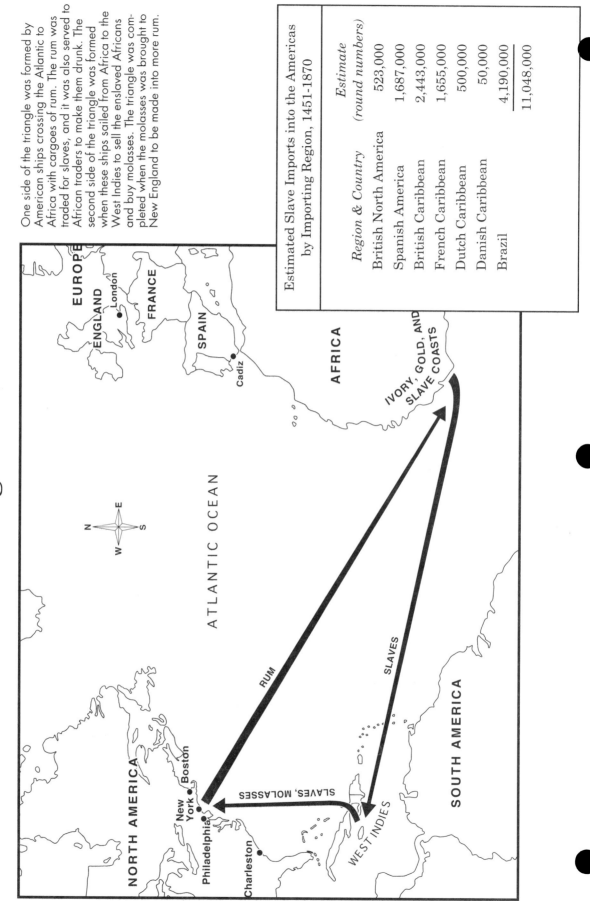

Estimated Slave Imports into the Americas by Importing Region, 1451–1870

Region & Country	Estimate (round numbers)
British North America	523,000
Spanish America	1,687,000
British Caribbean	2,443,000
French Caribbean	1,655,000
Dutch Caribbean	500,000
Danish Caribbean	50,000
Brazil	4,190,000
	11,048,000

New Orleans– A Center of Trade

Due to its location, New Orleans became an important trading center during the 1840s. Cotton and other agricultural goods were brought down the Mississippi River on steamboats. From there, these commodities were shipped to England and other European ports.

New Orleans was also an important port for the slave trade. However, New Orleans was known as a "cultured" city, so slave auctions were held out of public view. The slaves who were to be sold were kept in slave yards such as the one pictured below.

Engraving of a slave yard in New Orleans

The New York Public Library

Slave yards such as these were common in downtown New Orleans. It was illegal to display human merchandise on the sidewalks because ladies walking by might be offended. Traders tried to put a respectable face on their activity by dressing their male prisoners in suits and high hats. Nevertheless, a Danish visitor to a slave yard was not impressed. "I saw nothing especially repulsive in these places," she wrote, "excepting the whole thing."

A Surgeon's VIEWPOINT

Captives waiting to be shipped to America were held in barracoons, or slave barracks, like this one.

The Granger Collection

John Atkins was an 18th-century British naval surgeon. In the following excerpt from his writings, he offers advice to slave traders in West Africa.

Slaves differ in their Goodness; those from the Gold Coast are accounted best, being cleanest limbed, and more docible[1] by our Settlements than others; but then they are, for that very reason, more prompt to Revenge, and murder the Instruments of their Slavery, and also apter in the means to compass[2] it.

I have observed how our trading is managed for Slaves. . . . They are sold in open Market on shore, and examined by us in like manner, as our Brother Trade do Beasts in Smithfield, the Countenance, and Stature, a good Set of Teeth, Pliancy in their Limbs, and Joints . . . are the things inspected, and governs our choice in buying. . . .

Whydah Slaves are more subject to Small-Pox and sore Eyes; other parts to a sleepy Distemper.[3] . . . There are few instances of Deformity any where; even their Nobles know nothing of chronical Distempers, nor their Ladies of the Vapours.[4] Their flattish Noses are owing to a continued grubbing in their Infancy against their Mother's Backs.

---

[1] *docible*: docile, or teachable

[2] *compass*: accomplish

[3] *Distemper*: disease

[4] *the Vapours*: depressed spirits, a common ailment of upper-class women of the time

MEMORIES OF
AFRICA

Almost all the written accounts of slave trading are told from the traders' points of view. One exception is the autobiography of Olaudah Equiano, renamed Gustavus Vassa. Equiano was born around 1745. Captured by slavers at the age of ten, he was eventually shipped to Barbados, then to Virginia, and finally to England. In 1766 he purchased his freedom. For the rest of his life he worked for the abolition of the slave trade.

In the following excerpt from his autobiography, Equiano describes his homeland.

As we live in a country where nature is prodigal of her favours, our wants are few, and easily supplied; of course we have few manufactures. They consist for the most part of calicoes, earthen ware, ornaments, and instruments of war and husbandry. But these make no part of our commerce, the principal articles of which, as I have observed, are provisions. In such a state money is of little use; however we have some small pieces of coin, if I may call them such. They are made something like an anchor; but I do not remember either their value or denomination. We have also markets, at which I have been frequently with my mother. These are sometimes visited by stout mahogany-coloured men from the south-west of us; we call them Oye-Eboe,[1] which term signifies red men living at a distance. They generally bring us firearms, gunpowder, hats, beads, and dried fish. The last we esteemed a great rarity, as our waters were only brooks and springs. These articles they barter with us for odoriferous woods and earth, and our salt of wood-ashes. They always carry slaves through our land; but the strictest account is exacted of their manner of procuring them before they are suffered [allowed] to pass. Sometimes indeed we sold slaves to them, but they were only prisoners of war, or such among us as had been convicted of kidnapping, or adultery, and some other crimes, which we esteemed heinous. This practice of kidnapping induces me to think, that, notwithstanding all our strictness, their principal business among us was to trepan [entrap] our people. I remember too they carried great sacks along with them, which not long after I had an opportunity of fatally

Olaudah Equiano, renamed
Gustavus Vassa

The New York Public Library

---

[1] *Oye-Eboe*: an Ibo people living east of the Niger River

continued

19

seeing applied to that infamous purpose.

Our land is uncommonly rich and fruitful, and produces all kinds of vegetables in great abundance. We have plenty of Indian corn, and vast quantities of cotton and tobacco. Our pine apples grow without culture [farming]; they are about the size of the largest sugar-loaf, and finely flavoured. We have also spices of different kinds, particularly pepper; and a variety of delicious fruits which I have never seen in Europe; together with gums[2] of various kinds, and honey in abundance. All our industry is exerted to improve those blessings of nature. Agriculture is our chief employment; and every one, even the children and women, are engaged in it. Thus we are all habituated to labour from our earliest years. Every one contributes something to the common stock; and, as we are unacquainted with idleness, we have no beggars. The benefits of such a mode of living are obvious. The West India planters prefer the slaves of Benin or Eboe to those of any other part of Guinea, for their hardiness, intelligence, integrity, and zeal. Those benefits are felt by us in the general healthiness of the people, and in their vigour and activity; I might have added too in their comeliness. Deformity is indeed unknown amongst us, I mean that of shape. Numbers of the natives of Eboe, now in London, might be brought in support of this assertion; for, in regard to complexion, ideas of beauty are wholly relative. I remember while in Africa to have seen three negro children, who were tawny, and another quite white, who were universally regarded by myself and the natives in general, as far as related to their complexions, as deformed.

Our women too were, in my eyes at least, uncommonly graceful, alert, and modest to a degree of bashfulness; nor do I remember to have ever heard of an instance of incontinence amongst them before marriage. They are also remarkably cheerful. Indeed cheerfulness and affability are two of the leading characteristics of our nation.

> **Our land is uncommonly rich and fruitful, and produces all kinds of vegetables in great abundance.**
>
> **Olaudah Equiano**

[2] *gums*: probably rubber

CAPTURED!

In this excerpt, Samuel Ajayi Crowther describes how slave traders captured their prey. He also describes the pain of people who would never see one another again. Fortunately, the ship on which Crowther was held captive was caught by the British Navy, and he was set free.

The morning in which my town, Ocho-gu, shared the same fate which many others had experienced, was fair and delightful; and most of the inhabitants were engaged in their respective occupations. We were preparing breakfast without any apprehension; when, about 9 o'clock A.M., a rumour was spread in the town, that the enemies had approached with intentions of hostility. It was not long after when they had almost surrounded the town, to prevent any escape of the inhabitants; the town being rudely fortified with a wooden fence, about four miles in circumference, containing about 12,000 inhabitants, which would produce 3,000 fighting men. The inhabitants not being duly prepared, some not being at home; those who were, having about six gates to defend, as well as many weak places about the fence to guard against, and, to say in a few words, the men being surprised, and therefore confounded—the enemies entered the town after about three or four hours' resistance. Here a most sorrowful scene imaginable was to be witnessed!—women, some with three, four, or six children clinging to their arms, with the infants on their backs, and such baggage as they could carry on their heads, running as fast as they could through prickly shrubs, which, hooking their blies* and other loads, drew them down from the heads of the bearers. While they found it impossible to go along with their loads, they endeavoured only to save themselves and their children: even this was impracticable with those who had many children to care for. While they were endeavouring to disentangle themselves from the ropy shrubs, they were overtaken and caught by the enemies with a noose of rope thrown over the neck of every individual, to be led in the manner of goats tied together, under the drove of one man. In many cases a family was violently divided between three or four enemies, who each led his away, to see one another no more. Your humble servant was thus caught—with his mother, two sisters (one an infant about ten months old), and a cousin—while endeavouring to escape in the manner above described. My load consisted in nothing else than my bow, and five arrows in the quiver; the bow I had lost in the shrub, while I was extricating myself, before I could think of making any use of it against my enemies. The last view I had of my father was when he came from the fight, to give us the signal to flee: he entered into our house, which was burnt some time back for some offence given by my father's adopted son. Hence I never saw him more. —Here I must take thy leave, unhappy, comfortless father!—I learned, some time afterward, that he was killed in another battle.

Samuel Ajayi Crowther
Culver Pictures

* *blies*: nomadic hunters' loads

21

FROM A CAPTAIN'S LOG

Born in Italy, Theophilus Conneau eventually settled in Boston. He was captain of a slave ship from 1829 to 1847, when the trade was illegal. In the following excerpt from his log book, Conneau describes the stowing of slaves on board ship.

March 1827

Much has been said in regard to the stowing of Negroes on board of slavers, and the words "packing and piling" invariably used to denote the mode they are carried during the voyage. Permit me to describe this operation also, one of those forcible cruelties necessarily resorted to and inevitable on board a slaver.

    Two of the officers have the charge of stowing them. At sundown the second Mate and Boatswain descend, cat* in hand, and stow the Negroes for the night. Those on the starboard side face forward and in one another's lap, vulgarly called spoon fashion. On the port side they are stowed with face aft; this position is considered preferable for the free pulsation of the heart. The tallest are selected for the greatest breadth of the vessel, while the short size and youngsters are stowed in the fore part of the ship. Great precaution is also taken to place those such as may have sores or boils on the side most convenient for their distemper. Tubs are also distributed on the sleeping deck and so placed that both sides can have access. (The sick are never placed below.)

    . . . This discipline of stowing them is of the greatest importance on board slavers; otherwise every Negro would accommodate himself with all the comfortability of a cabin passenger.

---

* *cat*: cat-o'-nine-tails, whip made of nine knotted cords attached to a handle

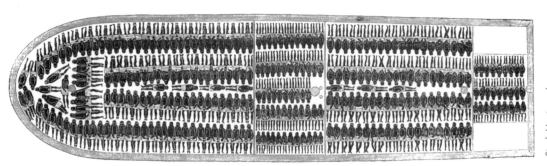

Diagram of the hold of a slave ship

ABOARD SHIP

There are few accounts of life on board a slave ship narrated by the captives themselves. The following description was written by Charles Ball, a slave whose grandfather was brought from Africa to the United States. As a boy, Charles listened to the stories of other slaves. In his autobiography, he recorded one slave's shipboard experiences.

At the time we came into this ship, she was full of black people, who were all confined in a dark and low place, in irons. The women were in irons as well as the men.

About twenty persons were seized in our village at the time I was; and amongst these were three children so young that they were not able to walk or to eat any hard substance. The mothers of these children had brought them all the way with them and had them in their arms when we were taken on board this ship.

When they put us in irons to be sent to our place of confinement in the ship, the men who fastened the irons on these mothers took the children out of their hands and threw them over the side of the ship into the water. When this was done, two of the women leaped overboard after the children—the third was already confined by a chain to another woman and could not get into the water, but in struggling to disengage herself, she broke her arm and died a few days after of a fever. One of the two women who were in the river was carried down by the weight of her irons before she could be rescued; but the other was taken up by some men in a boat and brought on board. This woman threw herself overboard one night when we were at sea.

The weather was very hot whilst we lay in the river and many of us died every day; but the number brought on board greatly exceeded those who died, and at the end of two weeks, the place in which we were confined was so full that no one could lie down; and we were obliged to sit all the time, for the room was not high enough for us to stand. When our prison could hold no more, the ship sailed down the river; and on the night of the second day after she sailed, I heard the roaring of the ocean as it dashed against her sides.

After we had been at sea some days, the irons were removed from the women and they were permitted to go upon deck; but whenever the wind blew high, they were driven down amongst us.

We had nothing to eat but yams, which were thrown amongst us at random—and of these we had scarcely enough to support life. More than one third of us died on the passage and when we arrived at Charleston, I was not able to stand. It was more than a week after I left the ship before I could straighten my limbs. I was bought by a trader with several others, brought up country and sold to my present master. I have been here five years.

SLAVE REVOLT

Captive Africans stage a successful revolt on the slave ship *Amistad*, 1839

Against great odds, the captives on slave ships occasionally revolted, usually unsuccessfully. In 1734 slave trader William Snelgrave wrote a book that included the following description of a slave revolt.

These Mutinies [slave revolts] are generally occasioned by the Sailors ill usage of these poor People, when on board the Ship wherein they are transported to our Plantations. . . .

The first Mutiny I saw among the Negroes, happened during my first Voyage, in the Year 1704. It was on board the Eagle Galley of London, commanded by my Father, with whom I was as Purser.[1] We had bought our Negroes in the River of Old Callabar in the Bay of Guinea. At the time of their mutinying we were in that River, having four hundred of them on board, and not above ten white men who were able to do Service; For several of our Ship's Company were dead, and many more sick; besides, two of our Boats were just then gone with twelve People on Shore to fetch Wood, which

lay in sight of the Ship. All these Circumstances put the Negroes on consulting how to mutiny, which they did at four a clock in the Afternoon, just as they went to Supper. But as we had always carefully examined the Mens Irons, both Morning and Evening, none had got them off, which in a great measure contributed to our Preservation. Three white Men stood on the Watch with Cutlaces[2] in their Hands. One of them was on the Forecastle, a stout fellow, seeing some of the Men Negroes take hold of the chief Mate, in order to throw him over board, he laid on them so heartily with the flat side of his Cutlace, that they soon quitted the Mate, who escaped from them, and run on the

[1] *Purser*: ship's officer in charge of accounts
[2] *Cutlaces*: short, curved swords

continued

Quarter Deck to get Arms. I was then sick with an Ague,[3] and laying on a Couch in the great Cabbin, the Fit being just come on. However, I no sooner heard the Outcry, That the Slaves were mutinying but I took two Pistols, and run on the Deck with them; where meeting with my Father and the chief Mate, I delivered a Pistol to each of them. Whereupon they went forward on the Booms, calling to the Negroe Men that were on the Forecastle; but they did not regard their Threats, being busy with the Centry, (who had dis-engaged the chief Mate), and they would have certainly killed him with his own Cutlace, could they have got it from him; but they could not break the Line Where-with the Handle was fastened to his Wrist. And so, tho' they had seized him, yet they could not make use of his Cutlace. Being thus disappointed, they endeavored to throw him overboard, but he held so fast by one of them that they could not do it. My Father seeing this stout Man in so much Danger, ventured amongst the negroes to save him; and fired his pistol over their Heads, thinking to frighten them. But a lusty Slave struck him with a Billet[4] so hard, that he was almost stunned. The Slave was going to repeat his Blow, when a young Lad about seventeen years old, whom we had been kind to, interposed his Arm, and received the Blow, by which his Arm-bone was fractured. At the same instant the Mate fired his Pistol, and shot the Negroe that had struck my Father. At the sight of this the Mutiny ceased, and all the Men-negroes on the Forecastle threw themselves flat on their Faces, crying out for Mercy. . . .

---

[3] *Ague*: fever marked by fits of chills
[4] *Billet*: wooden club

Slaves were forced to dance to keep them healthy and therefore marketable.

Dancing the Slaves

A Pictorial History of the Slave Trade by Isabelle Aguet
*contains graphic pictures of life on a slaver. It also presents this
firsthand account of how slavers made their captives dance.*

Each day they bring a certain number of Negroes up to the deck; they take off their irons, surround them with sentinels who guard them, gun in hand, and order them to dance the favorite dance of their country. Upon refusal from the Negroes, whips resound; their bodies are tortured to force them to dance. The most timid begin; the sailors encourage them with lashes of the whip and soon the dance becomes so alive and animated that it is difficult to make it stop. This spectacle is horrible to see. The Negro dancing in spite of himself, carried along in spite of himself by habit and pleasure, giving howls of horrible sensual delight which mix with the noise of the whips and the tom-tom, while men propped on the bulwarks are there to keep the blacks from throwing themselves into the sea; all that is hideous, all that is dreadful. . . . Then the Negroes take up their chains again and sadly go back to their cesspool, cursing their frantic joy of a moment and crying with rage for having succumbed to it.

Life of a Sailor

James Stanfield served for many years as a seaman aboard English slaving ships. Eventually, he was asked by an English Abolitionist to describe his experiences. The following excerpts are from Stanfield's letters, which were published in 1807.

During the first part of the passage, our allowance of water was three pints per day. For the last month it was reduced to one quart, wine measure. A quart of water in the torrid zone![1] . . . Happy used I to think myself, though almost fainting with fatigue, if a little sweat dropped from my forehead, that I might catch it in my mouth to moisten my parched tongue. The licking the dew off the hencoops in the morning had been long a delicious secret; but my monopoly was at last found out, and my little refreshment laid open to numbers. Many of the men could not refrain . . . from drinking up their whole allowance the moment they received it, and remained for the next four and twenty hours in a state of raging thirst not to be described. The doctor declared that this want of water, in such a climate and living entirely on salt provisions, must lead to the most fatal consequences.

During this scarcity with the men, the captain, besides plenty of beer and wine, had a large tea-kettle of water every morning, and another every evening, added to his allowance. . . .

It is unaccountable, but it is certainly true, that the moment a Guinea captain[2] comes in sight of this shore, the Demon cruelty seems to fix his residence within him. Soon after we arrived, there came on board us a master of a vessel, who was commissioned joint factor [trader] with our captain. All that I could conceive of barbarity fell short of the stories I heard of this man. His whole delight was in giving pain.

While our captain was placing buoys and other directions on the dangerous bar of the river for the purpose of crossing it, he [the other master] used to order the men to be flogged without an imputation [accusation] of the smallest crime. The steward, for serving out some red wine to the sick men, by the doctor's direction, was flogged in such a manner as not to be able to let his shirt touch his mangled back; and after his punishment, making an attempt to explain the matter, he was ordered to the shrouds again, and the same number of lashes was repeated.

It was his common practice to call his cabin boy to him, and without the slightest provocation, to tear his face, ears and neck, in the most brutal manner. I have seen him thrust his fingers into his [the cabin boy's] mouth and force them against the inside of his cheek till the wound appeared on the outside of the same. He had pulled his ears so much that they became of a monstrous size. The hind part of them was torn from the head. They had a continual soreness and running, and were not well near a twelve month after his infernal tormentor's death, when he [the cabin boy] deserted from us in the West Indies. . . .

In the following passages, Stanfield describes what happened when the captain and most of the crew fell ill.

The captain was so feeble that he could not move, but was obliged to be carried up and down. Yet his illness, so far from abating [decreasing] his tyranny, seemed rather to increase it. When in this situation, he has often asked the persons who carried him whether they could judge of the torment he was in? And being

[1] *torrid zone*: region between the tropics of Cancer and Capricorn
[2] *Guinea captain*: captain of a slave ship sailing to the area in Africa known as Guinea

continued

answered, no, he had laid hold of their faces and darting his nails into their cheeks with all his strength; on the person's crying out with the pain, he would then add, with the malignity [cruelty] of a demon, "There, that is to give you a taste of what I feel." . . .

The cook one day burned some meat in the roasting. He was called to the cabin on that account, and beaten most violently with the spit. He begged and cried for mercy, but without effect, until the strength of his persecutor was exhausted. He crawled somewhere—but never did duty afterwards. He died in a day or two.

The poor creatures [the crew], as our numbers thinned, were obliged to work when on the very verge of death. The certainty that they could not live a day longer, did not procure [obtain for] them a grain of mercy. The boatswain, who had left the coast a healthy hearty man, had been seized with the flux. He was in the last stage of it, but no remission [relief] from work was allowed him.

He grew so bad at last that the mucus, blood and whole strings of intestines came from him without intermission. Yet, even in this situation—when he could not stand—he was forced to the wheel, to steer a large vessel, an arduous [difficult]

duty, that in all likelihood would have required two men had we had people enough for the purpose. He was placed upon one of the mess-tubs, as not being able to stand, so that he might not dirty the deck. He remained at this painful duty as long as he could move his hands—he died on the same night. The body was, as usual, thrown overboard, without any covering but the shirt. It grew calm during the night and continued to be so for a good part of the next day—in the morning his corpse was discovered floating alongside and kept close to us for some hours—it was a horrid spectacle and seemed to give us the idea of the body of a victim calling out to heaven for vengeance on our barbarity.

In this state of weakness . . . little attention could be paid to those whose approach to the last stage of their misery renders [leaves] helpless and in want of aid. I remember that a man who was ill had one night crawled out of his hammock. He was so weak that he could not get back, but laid himself down on the gratings. . . . I shudder at the bare recollection he was still alive, but covered with blood—the hogs had picked his toes to the bone and his body was otherwise mangled by them in a manner too shocking to relate . . .

Sailors stowing captives on a slaver at night. Engraving by Henry Howe.

DISEASE ABOARD

Captive being forced overboard by sailors of a slave ship

The crowded and unsanitary conditions aboard slave ships often resulted in epidemics. When a disease struck, it affected enslaved Africans as well as the captain and crew. The following account describes an outbreak of an eye disease on a French slave ship in 1819. The story was supposedly written by a twelve-year-old French boy in a letter to his mother. His family had sent him on a slave ship to their plantation in the French West Indies. However, the accuracy of the account has been questioned.

It is now just a week since we sailed; but indeed, it is not my fault that I have not sooner sat down to write. The first two days I was sick, and the other five were so stormy that I could not sit at the table without holding. Even now we are rolling like a great porpoise yet I can sit very well and keep the pen steady. Since I am to send you what I do without copying it over again at the end of the voyage, I shall take what pains I can; but I hope, my dear mother, you will consider that my fingers are grown hard and tarry [covered with tar] with hauling all day on the ropes, the Captain being determined, as he says, to make me a sailor. . . .

All the slaves and some of the crew are blind. The Captain, the surgeon and the mate are blind. There is hardly enough men left out of our twenty-two, to work the ship. The Captain preserves what order he can and the surgeon still attempts to do his duty, but our situation is frightful.

All the crew are now blind but one man. The rest work under his orders like unconscious machines; the Captain standing by with a thick rope, which he sometimes applies, when led to any recreant [traitor] by the man who can see. My own eyes begin to be affected; in a little while, I shall see nothing but death. I asked the Captain if he would not allow the blacks to come up on deck. He said it was of no use; that the crew, who were always on deck, were as blind as they; that if brought up, they would only drown themselves, whereas, if they

continued

remained where they were, there would, in all probability, be at least a portion of them salable, if we ever had the good fortune to reach Guadaloupe.

We rolled along on our dreadful pain, with no other steersman than fate; for the single individual of the crew who was our last hope, now shares our calamity. . . .

Mother, your son was blind for ten days, although now so well as to be able to write. . . .

Then there came a storm. No hand was upon the helm, not a reef upon the sails. On we flew like a phantom ship of old, that cared not for wind or weather, our masts straining and cracking; our sails bursting from their bonds, with a report [sound] like that of musketry [guns]; the furious sea one moment devouring us up, stem and stern, and the next casting us forth again, as if with loathing and disgust. Even so did the whale cast forth Jonah. The wind, at last, died away and we found ourselves rocking, without progressive motion, on the sullen deep. We at length heard a sound upon the waters, unlike that of the smooth swell which remained after the storm, and our hearts beat with a hope which was painful from its suddenness and intensity. We held our breath. The sound was continued; it was like the splashing of a heavy body in smooth water; and a simultaneous cry arose from every lip on deck and was echoed by the men in their hammocks below and by the slaves in the hold.

Our cry was answered. . . .

"Ship Ahoy! Ahoy! What ship?"

"The *Saint Leon* of Spain. Help us for God's sake."

"We want help ourselves," replied our Captain.

"We are dying of hunger and thirst. Send us on board some provisions [food and drink] and a few hands to work the ship and name your own terms."

"We can give you food, but we are in want of hands. Come on board us and we will exchange provisions with you for men," answered our Captain.

"Dollars! Dollars! We will pay you in money, a thousand fold, but we cannot send anyone. We have negroes on board; they have infected us with ophthalmia, and we are all stone-blind."

At the announcement of this horrible coincidence, there was a silence among us, for some moments, like that of death. It was broken by a fit of laughter, in which I joined myself; and, after a moment, before our awful merriment was over, we could hear by the sound of the curses which the Spaniards shouted at us that the *Saint Leon* had drifted away.

The man who preserved his sight the longest recovered the soonest. To his exertions [work] alone, under the providence of God and the mercy of the blessed saints, is it owing that we are now within a few leagues of Guadaloupe, this twenty-second day of June 1819. I am myself almost well. The surgeon and eleven more are irrecoverably blind; the Captain has lost one eye; four others have met with the same calamity; and five are able to see, though dimly, with both. Among the slaves, thirty-nine are completely blind and the rest blind of one eye or their sight otherwise injured.

This morning the Captain called all hands on deck, negroes and all. The shores of Guadaloupe were in sight. I thought he was going to return God thanks publicly for our miraculous escape.

"Are you quite certain," said the mate, "that the cargo is insured?"

"I am," said the Captain. "Every slave that is lost must be made good by the underwriters [insurers]. Besides, would you have me turn my ship into a hospital for the support of blind negroes? They have cost us enough already. Do your duty."

The mate picked out thirty-nine negroes who were completely blind, and, with the assistance of the rest of the crew, tied a piece of ballast [weight] to the legs of each. The miserable wretches were then thrown into the sea.

An English Slave Trader Turned Abolitionist

AMAZING GRACE

"Amazing Grace" was written in 1789 by an ex-slave trader. John Newton had been the captain of a slave ship. He experienced a religious conversion and became a minister who frequently preached against slavery.

Amazing Grace! How sweet the sound
That saved a wretch like me!
I once was lost, but now am found,
Was blind, but now I see.

'Twas grace that taught my heart to fear,
And grace my fears relieved;
How precious did that grace appear
The hour I first believed!
Through many dangers, toils, and snares
I have already come;
'Tis grace that brought me safe thus far,
And grace will lead me home.

The Lord has promised good to me,
His word my hope secures;
He will my shield and portion be
As long as life endures.

The earth shall soon dissolve like snow,
The sun forbear to shine;
But God, who call'd me here below,
Will be forever mine.

Memories

In 1763, Newton wrote the following remembrance of his experience as a jailer on a slave ship.

I felt greatly the disagreeableness of the business. The office of a gaoler [jailer], and the restraints under which I was obliged to keep my prisoners, were not suitable to my feelings. But I considered the line of life which God in His providence had allotted me, as a cross which I ought to bear with patience and thankfulness till he should be pleased to deliver me from it. Till then I only thought myself bound to treat the slaves under my care with gentleness, and to consult their ease and convenience so far as was consistent with the safety of the whole family of whites and blacks on board my ship.

continued

Testimony

Later Newton made this statement as a witness before a parliamentary committee investigating the slave trade.

... I am bound in conscience to take shame to myself by a public confession, which, however sincere, comes too late to prevent or repair the misery and mischief to which I have formerly been accessory. I hope it always will be a subject of humiliating reflection to me that I was once an active instrument in a business at which my heart now shudders.

Perhaps what I have said of myself may be applicable to the nation at large. The slave trade was always unjustifiable. But inattention and interest prevented for a time the evil from being perceived. It is otherwise at present. The mischiefs and evils connected with it have been of late years represented with such undeniable evidence, and are now so generally known, that hardly an objection can be made to the almost universal wish for the suppression [end] of this trade, save [except] on the ground of political expedience [practicality].

Sermon

In 1797, Newton preached this sermon.

If the trade is at present carried on to the same extent and nearly in the same manner, while we are delaying from year to year to put a stop to our part in it, the blood of many thousands of our helpless, much injured fellow creatures is crying against us. The pitiable state of the survivors who are torn from their relatives, connections, and their native land must be taken into account. Enough of this horrid scene. I fear the African trade is a national sin, for the enormities which accompany it are now generally known.

Newton died in 1807, the year that England outlawed the slave trade.

AT AN AUCTION

*Slaves were often sold at public auctions. There children were frequently separated from their parents and husbands from their wives. Here is an eyewitness account of an auction that took place in Virginia in 1846. The excerpt is from **Eyewitness to History** edited by John Carey.*

We attended a sale of land and other property, near Petersburg, Virginia, and unexpectedly saw slaves sold at public auction. The slaves were told they would not be sold, and were collected in front of the quarters, gazing on the assembled multitude. The land being sold, the auctioneer's loud voice was heard, "Bring up the *niggers*!" A shade of astonishment and affright passed over their faces, as they stared first at each other, and then at the crowd of purchasers, whose attention was now directed to them. When the horrible truth was revealed to their minds that they were to be sold, and nearest relations and friends parted for ever, the effect was indescribably agonizing. Women snatched up their babes, and ran screaming into the huts. Children hid behind the huts and trees, and the men stood in mute despair. The auctioneer stood on the portico of the house, and the "men and boys" were ranging in the yard for inspection. It was announced that no warranty of *soundness* was given, and purchasers must examine for themselves. A few old men were sold at prices from thirteen to twenty-five dollars, and it was painful to see old men, bowed with years of toil and suffering, stand up to be the jest of brutal tyrants, and to hear them tell their disease and worthlessness, fearing that they would be bought by traders for the Southern market.

A white boy, about fifteen years old, was placed on the stand. His hair was brown and straight, his skin exactly the

Wilson Chinn, a branded slave from Louisiana, exhibiting instruments of torture used to punish slaves

Library of Congress

same hue as other white persons, and no discernible trace of negro features in his countenance [face].

Some vulgar jests were passed on his colour, and two hundred dollars were bid for him; but the audience said "that it was not enough to begin on for such a likely young nigger." Several remarked that they "would not have him as a gift." Some said a white nigger was more trouble than he was worth. One man said it was wrong to sell *white* people. I asked him if it was more wrong than to sell black people. He made no reply. Before he was sold, his mother rushed from the house upon the portico, crying in frantic grief, "My son, O!

continued

Engraving of a slave auction in the South before the Civil War

my boy, they will take away my dear–."
Here her voice was lost, as she was rudely
pushed back and the door closed. The sale
was not for a moment interrupted, and
none of the crowd appeared to be in the
least affected by the scene. The poor boy,
afraid to cry before so many strangers,
who showed no signs of sympathy or pity,
trembled, and wiped the tears from his
cheeks with his sleeves. He was sold for
about two hundred and fifty dollars.
During the sale, the quarters resounded
with cries and lamentations [sounds of
grief] that made my heart ache. A woman
was next called by name. She gave her
infant one wild embrace before leaving it

with an old woman, and hastened
mechanically to obey the call; but stopped,
threw her arms aloft, screamed, and was
unable to move.

One of my companions touched my
shoulder and said, "Come, let us leave
here; I can bear no more." We left the
ground. The man who drove our carriage
from Petersburg had two sons who
belonged to the estate—small boys. He
obtained a promise that they should not
be sold. He was asked if they were his
only children; he answered; "All that's left
of eight." Three others had been sold to
the South, and he would never see or hear
from them again.

VIEWPOINTS
on Slavery

The following quotations from various sources express a range of attitudes about slavery.

"... though liberty is a sweet thing to such as are born free, yet to those who may never know the sweets of it, slavery perhaps may not be so irksome. However this be, it is plain, to a demonstration, that hot countries can not be cultivated without Negroes. What a flourishing country might Georgia have been, had the use of them been permitted years ago!"
>—**George Whitefield,**
evangelist and preacher, 1751

"The colonists are by the law of nature freeborn, as indeed all men are, white or black. . . . Does it follow that 'tis right to enslave a man because he is black? . . . It is a clear truth that those who every day barter away other men's liberty will soon care little for their own."
>—**James Otis,** 1764

"I would never have drawn my sword in the cause of America if I could have conceived that thereby I was founding a land of slavery."
>—**Marquis de Lafayette**

"I never mean, unless some particular circumstances should compel me to it, to possess another slave by purchase, it being among my first wishes to see some plan adopted by which slavery in this country may be abolished by law."
>—**George Washington,**
in a letter dated September 9, 1786

The myth of the kind master and the grateful slave was kept alive for many years after emancipation by white southerners.

The New York Public Library

"Wo to this guilty land, unless she speedily repents of her evil doings! The blood of millions of her sons cries aloud for redress! IMMEDIATE EMANCIPATION can alone save her from the vengeance of Heaven, and cancel the debt of ages."
>—**William Lloyd Garrison,** 1831

"No human institution, in my opinion, is more manifestly consistent with the will of God than domestic slavery, and no one of His ordinances is written in more legible characters than that which consigns the African race to this condition, as more conducive to their own happiness, than any other of which they are susceptible."
>—**George McDuffie,**
governor of South Carolina, 1835

continued

"Never before has the black race of Central Africa, from the dawn of history to the present day, attained a condition so civilized and so improved, not only physically, but morally and intellectually. It came among us in a low, degraded, and savage condition, and in the course of a few generations it has grown up under the fostering care of our institutions, reviled as they have been, to its present comparatively civilized condition. This, with the rapid increase of the numbers, is conclusive proof of the general happiness of the race, in spite of all the exaggerated tales to the contrary."

—**John C. Calhoun,**
senator from South Carolina, 1837

". . . *slavery is alike the sin and the shame of the American people*: It is a blot upon the American name, and the only national reproach which need make an American hang his head in shame, in the presence of monarchical governments."

—**Frederick Douglass,** 1851

"At the slaveholding South all is peace, quiet, plenty and contentment. We have no mobs, no trade unions, no strikes for higher wages, no armed resistance to the law, but little jealousy of the rich by the poor."

"The slaves are all well fed, well clad, have plenty of fuel, and are happy. They have no dread of the future—no fear of want."

—**George Fitzhugh,**
Sociology for the South, 1854

"As I would not be a slave, so I would not be a master. This expresses my idea of democracy. Whatever differs from this, to the extent of the difference, is no democracy."

—**Abraham Lincoln,** 1858

"We were fed good and had plenty clothes to keep us dry and warm. . . . If all slaves had belonged to white folks like ours, there wouldn't been any freedom wanted."

—**Harriet McFarlin Payne,**
recorded in the 1930s

"Slavery was the worst days was ever seed in the world. They was things past telling, but I got the scars on my old body to show to this day. I seed worse than what happened to me."

—**Mary Reynolds,**
recorded in the 1930s

"Racial segregation, discrimination, and degradation are no unanticipated accidents in this nation's history. They stem logically and directly from the legacy that the Founding Fathers bestowed upon contemporary America. The denial of equality in the year of independence led directly to the denial of equality in the era of the bicentennial of independence."

—**John Hope Franklin,** 1975

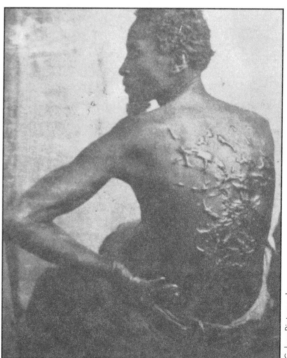

Culver Pictures, Inc.

Scars on the back of a former slave show the result of severe beatings.

36

In Their Own Words

Former slaves often narrated the stories of their lives. They recounted their captivity in interviews, essays, and full-length books. The following excerpts are from three of those narratives.

A Hundred Lashes

One day a heavy squall of wind and rain came on suddenly, and my mistress sent me round the corner of the house to empty a large earthen jar. The jar was already cracked with an old deep crack that divided it in the middle, and in turning it upside down to empty it, it parted in my hand. I could not help the accident, but I was dreadfully frightened, looking forward to a severe punishment. I ran crying to my mistress, "O mistress, the jar has come in two." "You have broken it, have you?" she replied; "come directly here to me." I came trembling; she stripped and flogged me long and severely with the cow-skin; as long as she had strength to use the lash, for she did not give over till she was quite tired.—When my master came home at night, she told him of my fault; and oh, frightful! how he fell a swearing. After abusing me with every ill name he could think of, (too, too bad to speak in England,) and giving me several heavy blows with his hand, he said, "I shall come home to-morrow morning at twelve, on purpose to give you a round hundred." He kept his word—Oh sad for me! I cannot easily forget it. He tied me up upon a ladder, and gave me a hundred lashes with his own hand, and master Benjy stood by to count them for him.

From *The History of Mary Prince, a West Indian Slave*

Dreadful Medicine

I have known the slaves to be so much fatigued from labor that they could scarcely get to their lodging places from the field at night. And then they would have to prepare something to eat before they could lie down to rest. Their corn they had to grind on a hand mill for bread stuff, or pound it in a mortar; and by the time they would get their suppers it would be midnight; then they would herd down all together and take but two or three hours rest, before the overseer's horn called them up again to prepare for the field.

At the time of sickness among slaves they had but very little attention. The master was to be the judge of their sickness, but never had studied the medical profession. He always pronounced a slave who said he was sick, a liar and a hypocrite; said there was nothing the matter, and he only wanted to keep from work.

His remedy was most generally strong red pepper tea, boiled till it was red. He would make them drink a pint cup full of it at one dose.

continued

If he should not get better very soon after it, the dose was repeated. If that should not accomplish the object for which it was given, or have the desired effect, a pot or kettle was then put over the fire with a large quantity of chimney soot, which was boiled down until it was as strong as the juice of tobacco, and the poor sick slave was compelled to drink a quart of it.

This would operate on the system like salts, or castor oil. But if the slave should not be very ill, he would rather work as long as he could stand up, than to take this dreadful medicine.

From *Narrative of the Life and Adventures of Henry Bibb,*
an American Slave

Hard Masters

Mrs. Flint, like many southern women, was totally deficient in energy. She had not strength to superintend her household affairs; but her nerves were so strong, that she could sit in her easy chair and see a woman whipped, till the blood trickled from every stroke of the lash. She was a member of the church; but partaking of the Lord's supper [communion] did not seem to put her in a Christian frame of mind. If dinner was not served at the exact time on that particular Sunday, she would station herself in the kitchen, and wait till it was dished, and then spit in all the kettles and pans that had been used for cooking. She did this to prevent the cook and her children from eking out their meagre fare with the remains of the gravy and other scrapings. The slaves could get nothing to eat except what she chose to give them. Provisions were weighed out by the pound and ounce, three times a day. I can assure you she gave them no chance to eat wheat bread from her flour barrel. She knew how many biscuits a quart of flour would make, and exactly what size they ought to be.

Dr. Flint was an epicure [lover of fine foods and drinks]. The cook never sent a dinner to his table without fear and trembling; for if there happened to be a dish not to his liking, he would either order her to be whipped, or compel her to eat every mouthful of it in his presence. The poor, hungry creature might not have objected to eating it; but she did object to having her master cram it down her throat till she choked.

They had a pet dog, that was a nuisance in the house. The cook was ordered to make some Indian mush for him. He refused to eat, and when his head was held over it, the froth flowed from his mouth into the basin. He died a few minutes after. When Dr. Flint came in, he said the mush had not been well cooked, and that was the reason the animal would not eat it. He sent for the cook, and compelled her to eat it. He thought that the woman's stomach was stronger than the dog's; but her sufferings afterwards proved that he was mistaken. This poor woman endured many cruelties from her master and mistress; sometimes she was locked up, away from her nursing baby, for a whole day and night.

From *Incidents in the Life of a Slave Girl*
by Harriet Jacobs

Frederick Douglass
Fights Back

Frederick Douglass

Frederick Douglass was born into slavery in Maryland around 1817. While enslaved he taught himself to read and write. In 1838, he escaped to freedom and soon became a leader in the movement to abolish slavery in the United States.

In 1845, Douglass published his autobiography, **Narrative of the Life of Frederick Douglass,** *from which the following excerpt is taken. In the passage, Douglass vividly recalls the moment when he realized that he was not powerless.*

Long before daylight, I was called to go and rub, curry, and feed, the horses. I obeyed, and was glad to obey. But whilst thus engaged, whilst in the act of throwing down some blades from the loft, Mr. Covey entered the stable with a long rope; and just as I was half out of the loft, he caught hold of my legs, and was about tying me. As soon as I found what he was up to, I gave a sudden spring, and as I did so, he holding to my legs, I was brought sprawling on the stable floor. Mr. Covey seemed now to think he had me, and could do what he pleased; but at this moment—from whence came the spirit I don't know—I resolved to fight; . . . I seized Covey hard by the throat; and as I did so, I rose. He held on to me, and I to him. My resistance was so entirely unexpected, that Covey seemed taken all aback. He trembled like a leaf. This gave me assurance, and I held him uneasy, causing the blood to run where I touched him with the ends of my fingers. Mr. Covey soon called out to Hughes for help. Hughes came, and, while Covey held me, attempted to tie my right hand. While he was in the act of doing so, I watched my chance, and gave him a heavy kick close under the ribs. This kick fairly sickened

continued

Hughes, so that he left me in the hands of Mr. Covey. This kick had the effect of not only weakening Hughes, but Covey also. When he asked me if I meant to persist in my resistance, I told him I did, come what might; that he had used me like a brute for six months, and that I was determined to be used so no longer. With that, he strove to drag me to a stick that was lying just out of the stable door. He meant to knock me down. But just as he was leaning over to get the stick, I seized him with both hands by his collar, and brought him by a sudden snatch to the ground. By this time, Bill came. Covey called upon him for assistance. Bill wanted to know what he could do. Covey said, "Take hold of him, take hold of him!" Bill said his master hired him out to work, and not to help to whip me; so he left Covey and myself to fight our own battle out. We were at it for nearly two hours. Covey at length let me go, puffing and blowing at a great rate, saying that if I had not resisted, he would not have whipped me half so much. The truth was, that he had not whipped me at all. I considered him as getting entirely the worst end of the bargain; for he had drawn no blood from me, but I had from him. The whole six months afterwards, that I spent with Mr. Covey, he never laid the weight of his finger upon me in anger. He would occasionally say, he didn't want to get hold of me again. "No," thought I, "you need not; for you will come off worse than you did before."

This battle with Mr. Covey was the turning-point in my career as a slave. It rekindled the few expiring embers of freedom, and revived within me a sense of my own manhood. It recalled the departed self-confidence, and inspired me again with a determination to be free. The gratification afforded by the triumph was a full compensation for whatever else might follow, even death itself. . . . I felt as I never felt before. It was a glorious resurrection, from the tomb of slavery, to the heaven of freedom. My long-crushed spirit rose, cowardice departed, bold defiance took its place; and I now resolved that, however long I might remain a slave in form, the day had passed forever when I could be a slave in fact. I did not hesitate to let it be known of me, that the white man who expected to succeed in whipping, must also succeed in killing me. . . .

> . . . . I felt as I never felt before. It was a glorious resurrection, from the tomb of slavery, to the heaven of freedom.
>
> **Frederick Douglass**

It was for a long time a matter of surprise to me why Mr. Covey did not immediately have me taken by the constable to the whipping-post, and there regularly whipped for the crime of raising my hand against a white man in defence of myself. And the only explanation I can now think of does not entirely satisfy me; but such as it is, I will give it. Mr. Covey enjoyed the most unbounded reputation for being a first-rate overseer and negro-breaker. It was of considerable importance to him. That reputation was at stake; and had he sent me—a boy about sixteen years old—to the public whipping-post, his reputation would have been lost; so, to save his reputation, he suffered me to go unpunished.

Voices from Other Novels

The following excerpts are from other novels about slavery or the slave trade.

The moans of the Foulah[1] shivered through the black hold. Then, after a while, a clear voice called out in Mandinka,[2] "Share his pain! We must be in this place as one village!" The voice belonged to an elder. He was right. The Foulah's pains had been as Kunta's own. He felt himself about to burst with rage. He also felt, in some nameless way, a terror greater than he had ever known before, and it seemed to spread from the marrow of his bones. Part of him wanted to die, to escape all of this; but no, he must live to avenge it. He forced himself to lie absolutely still. It took a long while, but finally he felt his strain and confusion, even his body's pains, begin to ebb—except the place between his shoulders where he had been burned with the hot iron. He found that his mind could focus better now on the only choice that seemed to lie before him and the others: Either they would all die in this nightmare place, or somehow the toubob [white men] would have to be overcome and killed.

—Roots
by Alex Haley

The barometer continued to fall. A swell rose next day, but no wind came. We should have been in Cuba by this time but in fact were little better than halfway there. And then they began to die. Two children went first. No telling what they died of, but it was up and over the side like bags of refuse. They floated astern for hours, with gulls wheeling and diving and making hoarse sounds of feasting. Their scabby legs skimmed the oily green water. After that there were deaths every day.

[1] *Foulah*: member of one West African group

[2] *Mandinka*: language spoken by many people in West Africa

Sharks began to follow us, and Mr. Gidding raved incessantly, as though money was being thrown away.

—So Ends This Day
by James Forman

Chinwe drifted toward her brother, who stared at the place where the sailors had jettisoned [thrown overboard] the dead man's body. Chinwe said, "Odili?"

"What is it?"

"This voyage will not go on forever. The doctor says it will end in a month, but before it ends, more men will die."

"Why are so many sick, Chinwe?"

"They lie together like fish in a basket, chained to a cable and to each other. The spirits of most of them are low. Some of them simply want to die."

"Will we ever go home?"

"I hope so, Odili."

"If we do, do you think we can find our father?"

"Yes, though it might take many months. Father is known throughout our land and many other lands as well."

—Chinwe
by Peter Burchard

Dondo pointed toward the sea.

"Slave ships," he said. "They're waiting for us."

There were three of them where the river met the sea. Three ships that needed paint were anchored a good distance from each other. All had tattered flags flying from their masts.

As we passed the first of the ships, blacks called down to us. With raised fists they warned us of the evils to come. They told us to jump into the sea. Some told us to kill our captors before it was too late.

—My Name Is Not Angelica
by Scott O'Dell

continued

41

"Cinque is here, and Tua, and the one they call Fulway. They want to sail the *Amistad* back to their own country. They want you to show them how to sail a ship. They bid me say they are here peacefully to have palaver [talk] with you."

"Palaver the devil!" Ruiz snorted.

"They say they will show you the way, by the sun," Antonio continued.

There was tumult in the cabin. Montez' voice rose shrilly. "To Africa! I'll not do it, though they kill me and cut me in pieces and feed me to the sharks."

Antonio cajoled [coaxed], "They say it is right that they should go to their homes. They want the ship turned to the sun." The boy felt Tua's fingers pressing into his arm. He fell silent to hear what Ruiz was saying. Suddenly he flattened himself against the wall. "They are going to shoot."

—***The Long Black Schooner***
by Emma Gelders Sterne

"I'm running away—Uncle Tom and Aunt Chloe—carrying off my child—Master sold him!"

"Sold him?" echoed both, lifting up their hands in dismay.

"Yes, sold him!" said Eliza, firmly; "I crept into the closet by Mistress' door to-night, and I heard Master tell Missis that he had sold my Harry, and you, Uncle Tom, both to a trader; and that he was going off this morning on his horse, and that the man was to take possession today."

—***Uncle Tom's Cabin***
by Harriet Beecher Stowe

October 1835

Dear Uncle Stephen,
This is the truth from my heart, from here to glory: I dont blame you, and I hope you dont blame Yourself. From where I sit, I say freedom is worth any price. but I am sorry the price you got to pay is never seeing Aunt Betty again.

Gran whispers through the trapdoor last night that Betty is beside herself. When Mister B's ship come home without you yesterday, she almost faint dead away. She is full of grief, and I wish I could go to her.

But nobody knows I'm up here, except Gran and Uncle Mark. When Norcom put Mark in jail, he threatened to torture him to find out where I was. So, to protect Betty, they wont tell her till it's safe. And the children, they cant never suspect their Mama is a-laying up under the roof in a space no bigger than a few coffins.

—***Letters from a Slave Girl:
The Story of Harriet Jacobs***
by Mary E. Lyons

From
The Women of Plums

__The Women of Plums,__ by Dolores Kendrick, is subtitled __Poems in the Voices of Slave Women.__ Though it was written by a contemporary African-American woman, it brings to life the feelings of enslaved women from the distant past.

To Market, to Market

Arthur Mason's Shopping List,
November 6, 1804

One Black Angus
One Yew
two Hogs
one Spinning Wheel
one Dresser Mirror
one nigger wench & child
(pay no more than $2,000)
twelve Silver Spoons
four Tea Cups
four saucers
four China Plates
one Pewter Tea-pot

Bill to be paid in full to
Tydus Wellington, sixth of November,
eighteen hundred and four.

From

Generations

Generations is poet Lucille Clifton's love song to her family. In the following excerpt, she recalls how her father used to tell her about his great-grandmother, Mammy Ca'line. She was born in Africa and brought to America on a slave ship.

Mammy Ca'line

"Mammy Ca'line raised me," Daddy would say. "After my Grandma Lucy died, she took care of Genie and then took care of me. She was my great-grandmother, Lucy's Mama, you know, but everybody called her Mammy like they did in them days. Oh she was tall and skinny and walked straight as a soldier, Lue. Straight like somebody marching wherever she went. And she talked with a Oxford accent! I ain't kidding. Don't let nobody tell you them old people was dumb. She talked like she was from London England and when we kids would be running and hooping and hollering all around she would come to the door and look straight at me and shake her finger and say 'Stop that Bedlam, mister, stop that Bedlam, I say.' With a Oxford accent, Lue! She was a dark old skinny lady and she raised my Daddy and then raised me, least till I was eight years old when she died. When I was eight years old. I remember everything she ever told me, cause you know when you that age you old enough to remember things. I remember everything she told me, Lue, even though she died when I was eight years old. And then I knowed about what she remembered cause that's how old she was when she got here. Eight years old."

SONGS OF SURVIVAL

Enslaved African Americans had few means to express themselves. But one strong tradition they carried with them from Africa was music. Combining the music of their homeland with the message of Christianity, African Americans created the spiritual.

Many spirituals focus on the joy of freedom to be achieved in the afterlife. However, they also express the desire to escape from slavery in the here and now. Frequent references to chariots, trains, ships, and crossing rivers are metaphors for escaping from slavery. Here are some of the most famous spirituals.

Swing Low, Sweet Chariot

(Refrain)
Swing low, sweet chariot,
Comin' for to carry me home!
Swing low, sweet chariot,
Comin' for to carry me home.

I looked over Jordan, an' what did I see,
Comin' for to carry me home!
A band of angels comin' after me,
Comin' for to carry me home.
(Refrain)

If you get there before I do,
Comin' for to carry me home!
Jes' tell my fren's that I'm a comin' too,
Comin' for to carry me home.
(Refrain)

I'm sometimes up an' sometimes down,
Comin' for to carry me home!
But still my soul feels heavenly boun'
Comin' for to carry me home.
(Refrain)

Roll, Jordan

Oh, roll, Jordan, roll!
Roll, Jordan, roll,
I want to go to heav'n when I die,—
To hear sweet Jordan roll.

Oh, brother, you ought to be there,
Oh, sister, you ought to be there,
Yes, my Lord, A-
Oh, Preacher, you'd Better be there,
sittin' in the kingdom,
Just to hear sweet Jordan roll.

continued

45

I Want to Die Easy

I want to die easy when I die;
I want to die easy when I die;
I want to die easy when I die;
Shout salvation as I fly,
I want to die easy when I die.

2. I want to see my mother . . .
3. I want to see my Jesus . . .

Let Us Break Bread Together

Let us break bread together on our knees.
Let us break bread together on our knees.
When I fall down on my knees with my face to the rising sun,
Oh, Lord have mercy on me.

Let us drink wine together on our knees.
Let us drink wine together on our knees.
When I fall down on my knees with my face to the rising sun,
Oh, Lord have mercy on me.

Let us praise God together on our knees.
Let us praise God together on our knees.
When I fall down on my knees with my face to the rising sun,
Oh, Lord have mercy on me.

Suggested Reading and Viewing List

*If you enjoyed reading **The Slave Dancer,** you may want to explore other related works. The following list offers suggestions for further reading and viewing.*

Novels

The Abduction by Mette Newth. Based on the actual kidnapping of Inuit Eskimos by European traders in the 17th century. This story describes the violence and cruelty inflicted in the name of civilization. Farrar, Straus & Giroux, 1989. [RL 7 IL 9-12]

I, Juan de Pareja by Elizabeth Borton De Trevino. The story of Juan, a slave, and his master, the Spanish painter Velázquez. Their relationship changes from master and slave to friend and equal. Farrar, Straus & Giroux, 1987. [RL 7 IL 6-12]

Jump Ship to Freedom by James Lincoln Collier and Christopher Collier. Although Daniel Arabus should be free by law, he finds himself on a ship headed for the West Indies and a life of slavery. Delacorte, 1981. [RL 5.5 IL 3-6]

Listen, Children: An Anthology of Black Literature edited by Dorothy S. Strickland. An introduction to the world of black literature, this collection celebrates the joy and pain of being young and black. Bantam, 1986. [RL 5 IL 6-12]

My Name Is Not Angelica by Scott O'Dell. A compelling account of the slave rebellion of 1733 and one young woman's suffering, strength, and ultimate triumph. Dell, 1990. [RL 5.5 IL 4-7]

Saturnalia by Paul Fleischman. Strands of several different stories are woven around that of William, an enslaved Narragansett Indian boy working as an apprentice in 1861 Boston. HarperCollins, 1990. [RL 6 IL 7-12]

The Slave Ship by Emma Gelders Sterne. Based on an actual episode in history, this is the saga of a group of Africans who take command of a slave schooner and attempt to return home. Scholastic, 1988. [RL 5 IL 3-7]

So Ends This Day by James Foreman. Set in the 1840s, this story recounts the events of a young boy's first voyage aboard his father's whaler. They eventually get involved in the slave trade. Farrar, Straus & Giroux, 1970. [RL 7 IL 7-10]

Voyage of the Frog by Gary Paulsen. Fourteen-year-old David intends to grant his uncle's last wish when he sets sail on the *Frog*. During the voyage, he faces many challenges. Dell, 1990. [RL 6 IL 6-12]

Wandering Girl by Glenyse Ward. The story of a young Australian Aboriginal woman's childhood as a domestic slave. Fawcett, 1991. [RL 7 IL 7-12]

The Whipping Boy by Sid Fleischman. A bratty prince and his whipping boy trade places after becoming involved with dangerous outlaws. A Newbery Medal winner. Morrow, 1986. [RL 3 IL 3-7]

continued

47

Nonfiction

Amos Fortune, Free Man by Elizabeth Yates. The true and inspirational story of one man committed above all to serving his fellow citizens—both African and American. A Newbery Medal winner. Penguin, 1989. [RL 5 IL 5-8]

The Black Americans: A History in Their Own Words by Milton Meltzer. Covering almost three centuries, this work features selections from letters, speeches, and memoirs of African Americans. Harper and Row, 1987. [RL 8.5 IL 7-12]

Black Dance in America: A History Through Its People by James Haskins. This book chronicles the evolution of African-American dance, from early slave dances to jazz and break dancing. HarperCollins, 1990. [RL 6 IL 6-12]

Black Voyage: Eyewitness Accounts of the Atlantic Slave Trade by Thomas Howard. First-person stories of the slave trade, told by sailors, captains, doctors, and enslaved people themselves. Little, Brown, 1971. [RL 8.5 IL 7-12]

Breaking the Chains: Afro-American Slave Resistance by William Loren Katz. This volume presents inspiring true stories of the heroism of American slaves prior to and during the Civil War. It tells the stories of people who were determined to live free or die. Atheneum, 1990. [RL 6 IL 6-9]

Bullwhip Days: The Slaves Remember edited by James Mellon. These narratives tell an unforgettable story of the horrors of life under slavery. Avon, 1989. [RL 8.5 IL 9+]

Rum, Slaves and Molasses: The Story of New England's Triangular Trade by Clifford Alderman. Traces the purchase, transport, and fate of Africans who fell victim to the New England slave trade with the West Indies. Cromwell-Collier, 1972. [RL 6 IL 6-10]

To Be a Slave by Julius Lester. The horrifying true story of slavery in America, told by the people who suffered its injustices. Scholastic, 1986. [RL 5 IL 6-12]

Up from Slavery by Booker T. Washington. The inspiring true story of a man who was born a slave but became a great educator and the founder of the Tuskegee Institute. Airmont, 1986. [RL 6 IL 7-12]

Poetry

"Afro-American Fragment" by Langston Hughes

I Am the Darker Brother: An Anthology of Poems by Negro Americans edited by Arnold Adoff. Over 60 poems by 28 outstanding black writers. Macmillan, 1968. [RL 6 IL 6-12]

"If We Must Die" by Claude McKay

Videos

The Autobiography of Miss Jane Pittman. This award-winning film tells the life story of the fictional Jane Pittman, who is born a slave but lives to see the civil rights movement of the 1960s. CBS. (VHS, color, 120 minutes)

Black History in America. This five-part series explores 400 years of black American history, from slavery to Jesse Jackson's presidential candidacy. Educational Design. (VHS, color, 84 minutes each)

continued

Half Slave, Half Free. The dramatic true story of Solomon Northup, born and raised as a free man in New York State. Captured and sold, he endured the horrors of slavery for 12 years before escaping to the North. Blacast Productions. (VHS, color, 119 minutes)

Roots: The Triumph of an American Family. The struggle of African Americans for freedom and dignity is illustrated through the telling of one family's odyssey. ABC-TV. (VHS, color, 12 hours)

Slavery: America's Peculiar Institution. This two-part program examines slavery as it was practiced in the United States. Part One traces the capture of slaves in Africa and their transport to North America. Part Two examines the lives of slaves, including their work, living conditions, and family relationships. Zenger. (VHS, color, each 32 minutes)

Using Latitudes in Your Classroom

*The following discussion topics and activities are suggestions for incorporating pieces from **Latitudes** into your curriculum. Most suggestions can be adapted for independent, small group, or whole class activities. In addition, the list includes activities that can be done before, during, and after reading the novel. The variety of choices allows you to modify and use those activities that will make **The Slave Dancer** meaningful to your students.*

About the Author

1. Paula Fox moved often as a child and young adult. Discuss with students whether they think such a life has helped Fox as a writer. Ask them to predict the kind of writing they might expect from Fox.
2. Paula Fox has some Irish ancestry. Interested students might want to research the Irish migration to America. In particular, they might want to investigate the system of indentured servitude mentioned by Purvis in *The Slave Dancer*.
3. Fox mentions that she wrote *The Slave Dancer* to show the effects of slavery upon the enslaver. After students read the book, ask them if Fox meets this goal. Have students substantiate their responses with examples from the book.

Critics' Comments

1. Invite students to speculate about whether Paula Fox has the necessary experience to write a novel about the slave trade. As students respond, encourage them to provide valid arguments for their position. You might prompt students with the following statements. Ask students to indicate whether they agree or disagree with each one.
   • Writers should stick to subjects within their personal experience.
   • Those most sensitive to injustice are those most harmed by it. Therefore, books about injustice (such as slavery) should be written by people who have suffered similar injustice in their lives.
   • Authors should be free to write about any topic that interests them.
2. As students read the novel, invite them to keep a reader's journal in which they note passages that they like or dislike. Have them write short responses explaining their feelings.
3. Julius Lester objects to *The Slave Dancer* for several reasons. After students have read the novel, ask them if they agree with the following statements by Lester.
   • "As a character, Jessie simply is not interesting."
   • "[Jessie] becomes a mere device for the transmission of information about life on a slave ship and the slave trade."
   • "Throughout the novel [Jessie] is passive, accepting his own capture with scarcely a word of protest and even developing a warm affection for Purvis, one of his kidnappers."
   • "The Africans are depicted as rather pathetic and dumb creatures, so much so in fact that it is difficult to have sympathy for them."

continued

- "This novel describes the horrors of the Middle Passage, but it does not re-create them, and if history is to become a reality, the reader must live that history as if it were his own life."
4. Invite students to write their own critical statements about *The Slave Dancer*. Some students might take issue with Lester's or Fox's comments. Remind them to support their opinions with evidence from the book. Then around the room, post unsigned comments written on large sheets of paper. The class can discuss the different reactions.

Voices from the Novel

1. After students have read the excerpts, have them predict the conflicts in the novel and how these might be resolved.
2. As students read, encourage them to make notes of other significant passages in the novel that reflect a central idea or theme. As a follow-up, students could write essays explaining the significance of one of the quotations they chose.
3. Discuss with students the effect of having the story told by Jessie Bollier. Have them speculate how the novel would have been different if it had been told by one of the other characters.
4. Discuss with students modern issues that are similar to those raised in the novel.

A Time in History

1. Note with students the historical events on the timeline. Encourage them to use the library to find more information about each event. Then challenge students to think about how those happenings might have been viewed by the following people.
   - an enslaved African
   - a slaveholder
   - the captain of a slave ship
   - a sailor on a slave ship
2. As students read the novel, have them add to the timeline historical events mentioned in the story.
3. Interested students might research significant events in West Africa from 1619 to 1865 and present their findings in a timeline.

The Geographical Picture

1. Before students read the novel, have them review the map of the triangular trade. Ask them to locate the route a slave ship might take from New Orleans to Africa.
2. As students read the novel, suggest that they record information about the following topics.
   - people who profited by the slave trade
   - Spanish and Portuguese involvement in the slave trade
   - the role of Cuba in the North American slave trade
   - policing of the slave trade by British and American ships
   As a follow-up, student groups could do further research and prepare a report on one of the above topics.

continued

3. Interested students may want to investigate why so much of the slave trade took place on the western coast of Africa.
4. Ask students to form groups and respond to the following questions.
   • What immoral economic activities do people engage in today?
   • Why do people engage in these activities?
   • What can be done to address these problems?

New Orleans—A Center of Trade

1. Have students investigate New Orleans in the 1840s. You might use some of the following questions as prompts.
   • Were there places in the United States where the sale of slaves was outlawed?
   • In 1840, were there laws against the importation of slaves from Africa? (Students could consult the timeline for this information.)
   • Why did New Orleans become the biggest slave market in the South?
   • What regulations, sanctions, or punishments were used to make sure that laws against the importation of slaves were being followed?
   • Did the United States government attempt to stop the importation of slaves? How?
2. Ask students why "cultured" people might be offended by the sight of captives being sold into slavery. Interested students may want to research ways that slaveholders rationalized the institution of slavery.

A Surgeon's Viewpoint

1. Before they read this selection, ask students to list behaviors that make them feel as if they are being treated disrespectfully. After students have read the selection, help them analyze the surgeon's attitude toward the "human cargo."
2. After students have read this selection, invite them to contrast the slaver's perspective with the feelings of his captives. (You might refer students to "Memories of Africa" and "Captured!" for the captives' perspective.) Invite students to compare this account to the novel.
3. Interested students might find other first-person accounts of slave voyages. Several are available in *Black Voyage* edited by Thomas Howard.

Memories of Africa/Captured!

1. Before students read "Memories of Africa," ask if they think all slave traders were from Europe or America. As students read this selection, ask them to look for evidence that some Africans were active in the slave trade.
2. Remind students that supporters of slavery often argued that slaves lived better than their relatives in Africa. After students have read these selections, ask them to describe how the authors lived in their native countries. Discuss whether these selections support the

continued

argument that slaves were better off in the care of their masters than in "uncivilized" Africa.

3. After reading both selections, students might discuss ways in which Africans resisted slavers.

4. The full autobiography of Olaudah Equiano is available in *The Classic Slave Narratives* edited by Henry Louis Gates, Jr., and *Africa Remembered: Narratives by West Africans from the End of the Slave Trade* edited by Philip D. Curtin. Interested students might read other parts of the autobiography and report on it to the class.

5. Interested students might investigate whether slavery is still practiced in any countries today.

From a Captain's Log

1. Explain to students that a ship's log was used to keep a daily record of the ship's progress and the routine activities on board. As a pre-reading exercise, have students keep a log of their own activities for one day or a morning. Have students attempt to exclude feelings from their log. They should only describe physical actions.

2. Captain Conneau mentions that "packing and piling" the enslaved Africans was "one of those forcible cruelties necessarily resorted to and inevitable on board a slaver." Discuss with students the attitude that the captain has toward the suffering experienced by the Africans. The following questions might help students analyze Conneau's language.
   • Is there any indication that Captain Conneau is concerned about the feelings of the Africans?
   • Why does the captain want his cargo to remain healthy?
   • How would a person who was against the slave trade describe the packing of the enslaved Africans? As a follow-up, you might invite students to rewrite Captain Conneau's description from the perspective of a person who viewed slavery as immoral.

3. Interested students might want to contrast the forced migration of Africans across the Middle Passage with other migrations. The migrations of the following groups might be of interest.
   • the *Mayflower* pilgrims
   • the Irish to America during the potato famine
   • Vietnamese boat people
   • Haitian boat people

Aboard Ship

1. Discuss with students the importance of storytelling in passing on traditional values and beliefs in African cultures. Ask them to name stories that teach values of their own culture.

2. As students read the novel, have them compare Fox's description of the Middle Passage with the description given in "Aboard Ship."

3. Interested students may want to investigate the mythology and storytelling traditions of one of the western African cultures, such as the Yoruba or Ashanti. (See *Retold African Myths* by Eleanora Tate for stories and background information.) Then invite students to retell *The Moonlight*'s voyage to Cuba from the perspective of Ras or one of the other enslaved Africans.

continued

Slave Revolt

1. Before students read this selection, ask them to list the dangers of early transatlantic voyages. Then have them use information from the selection to expand their list.
2. After students have read this selection, invite them to react to this comment by Abraham Lincoln: "When . . . you have succeeded in dehumanizing the Negro; when you have put him down and made it impossible for him to be but as the beasts of the field, . . . are you quite sure that the demon you have roused will not turn and rend [break or tear] you?" You might use the following questions to prompt responses.
   • How were the captives "dehumanized"?
   • Could the slavers have been active in the slave trade if they saw their captives as fully human?
   • How do people react to having their rights taken away?
3. Ask students to imagine what would have happened if the Africans on *The Moonlight* had rebelled. Have them write a new chapter for the book describing a slave revolt.
4. Interested students might research the successful slave revolt on *The Amistad* in 1839 and share their findings with the class.

Dancing the Slaves

1. Before students read this selection, inform them that African dance forms were very different from 19th-century European forms. You might find illustrations or photographs of traditional West-African dances to illustrate this point. Then ask students if the writer of "Dancing the Slaves" interpreted the Africans' behavior correctly. You might have students look closely at the following passages.
   • "The Negro dancing in spite of himself, carried along . . . by habit and pleasure, giving howls of horrible sensual delight . . ."
   • "Then the Negroes take up their chains again . . . cursing their frantic joy of a moment and crying with rage for having succumbed to it."
2. As students read the novel, have them compare Fox's description of dancing the slaves with this account. Which seems more believable?
3. Interested students might want to investigate further the dance traditions of western Africa. They could prepare a report or bulletin board display of their findings.

Life of a Sailor

1. Have students chart situations in this selection and in the novel in which cruelty becomes accepted as a part of life. You might want to create a two-column chart in which you list the behavior in one column and the justification for the behavior in the second column. Have students speculate on ways to break such cycles of cruelty.
2. As students read, ask them to compare Stanfield's experience to the experiences of the sailors in *The Slave Dancer*. Students could note parts of the novel that closely correspond to Stanfield's account. Then have students decide whether Fox's novel seems historically accurate.

continued

3. Interested students may investigate further the lives of sailors. Students could try to find the answers to the following questions.
   • Was the brutal treatment of sailors described by Stanfield common?
   • What recourse did sailors have against brutal treatment?
   • What were common causes of mutinies?
   • Given the treatment of sailors described by Stanfield, why weren't there more mutinies?

Disease Aboard

1. Ask students whether they think the events described in this letter really happened. Have students indicate the parts of the story that seem believable and the parts that don't. Students should use evidence from the story to substantiate their views.
2. Have students imagine what other legends the transatlantic slave trade might have inspired. Interested students might want to investigate other sailing legends.
3. Interested students could investigate other diseases common to sailors.

An English Slave Trader Turned Abolitionist/ At an Auction

1. John Newton says that being in the slave trade was "a cross to bear." He also felt obliged to remain in the trade because it was "the line of life which God in His providence has allotted me." Have students write Newton a letter explaining their response to his statements. Students should try to explain why they agree or disagree with Newton's attitude.
2. As students read the novel, have them watch for characters who use arguments similar to Newton's for being a slave trader.
3. After leaving the slave trade, Newton became a minister and worked to abolish slavery. Have students speculate about his probable success in influencing others. Would Newton have been more effective than someone who had not been a slaver? Students might want to analyze Newton's song "Amazing Grace" for evidence of his success.
4. Invite students to compare Newton's writings and song to the eyewitness account of the slave sale in "At an Auction." Ask students to choose the piece they feel is more powerful. Have them explain their choice.

Viewpoints on Slavery

1. With students, categorize and chart the various viewpoints on slavery. What arguments are made against and in support of slavery? Compare and contrast the feelings expressed. Why might each person have that particular viewpoint?

continued

2. As students read the novel, have them categorize and chart the main characters according to their viewpoints on the slave trade. These views could be added to the chart made for the preceding activity. After students finish the novel, encourage them to compare their charts with those of other students and discuss the variety of viewpoints in the novel.

3. Ask students to select a viewpoint and write an essay that supports or disputes the view expressed.

In Their Own Words

1. After reading these three passages, ask students if they can identify any limits to the power slaveholders had over their human "property."

2. As students read the novel, have them compare the attitudes of the slaveholders with Captain Cawthorne's attitude toward his human cargo. What excuses might the slaveholders give for treating human beings in this fashion?

3. In pairs, have students explain how one of the following scenes would have been different if Jessie Bollier had been the son of a slaveholder.
   • Jessie's introduction to the captain and crew of *The Moonlight*
   • the loading of the captured Africans on *The Moonlight*
   • Jessie and Ras on the beach together

Frederick Douglass Fights Back

1. Discuss with students the characteristics that Frederick Douglass displayed in this episode. How might these characteristics have served him in his escape from slavery? in his efforts to abolish slavery?

2. As students read the novel, suggest that they watch for places where a character either fights oppression or gives in to it. Challenge students to indicate how the scene might have gone had Frederick Douglass been the character in question.

3. Julius Lester indicates in his critique of *The Slave Dancer* that the Africans "are depicted as rather pathetic and dumb creatures, so much so in fact that it is difficult to have sympathy for them." Have students compare Frederick Douglass' response to oppression with Paula Fox's descriptions of the Africans. Ask students if they think Lester's critique is valid.

Voices from Other Novels

1. With students, cluster or map similar themes or conflicts in the quoted novels. Ask students to consider why so many books have been written on these themes.

2. Encourage students to select and write about the connections they see between *The Slave Dancer* and the quoted books.

3. Interested students may want to read one of the books quoted and prepare a report for the class.

continued

From *The Women of Plums*

1. Discuss with students the effect the poet creates by placing "one nigger wench & child" in the middle of the shopping list.
2. Have students compare the dehumanizing language of this poem to the attitude of Captain Cawthorne in *The Slave Dancer* or the language of the surgeon in "A Surgeon's Viewpoint."
3. Have students write their own poems in the voice of Ras or one of the other enslaved Africans in *The Slave Dancer*. Provide time for them to read their poems to the class.

From *Generations*

1. Ask students to imagine that they could interview Mammy Ca'line about her experiences before, during, and after slavery. Suggest that they use the information in the excerpt to imagine how she would answer their questions.
2. Students might write a short piece similar to the excerpt from *Generations*. Have them write it from the perspective of a descendant of Ras or Daniel.
3. Invite interested students to read the rest of *Generations* and present a report to the class.

Songs of Survival

1. Have students paraphrase the songs. What might these songs be saying about slavery and freedom?
2. At the end of *The Slave Dancer*, Jessie says that he cannot listen to music. Ask the students if they think he would have been able to listen to "Swing Low, Sweet Chariot" or "Let Us Break Bread Together." Have them explain their responses.
3. Interested students might find recordings of these or other spirituals and play them for the class.

Student Projects

The suggestions below will help you extend your learning about slavery and the slave trade. The categories give choices for reading, writing, speaking, and visual activities. You are also encouraged to design your own project.

The Historian's Study

1. Find out more about the history and culture of West Africa, the area from which many Africans were brought to the Americas as slaves. The following are some major groups of West Africans.
   - Ashanti
   - Bambara
   - Dugou
   - Fulani
   - Hausa
   - Ibo
   - Yoruba

2. Research slavery in other cultures and present your findings in a written report. You could research the following cultures:
   - Roman
   - Egyptian
   - Aztec
   - Native American
   - Islamic

3. Find out more about the lives of sailors in the first half of the 18th century and present your findings to the class.

4. Other topics for research:
   - the first Africans to come to the Americas
   - rebellions against slavery in the United States, including those led by Nat Turner, Denmark Vesey, and John Brown
   - life on Southern plantations for the enslaved and the enslavers
   - Toussaint L'Ouverture and the revolt of Haiti's slaves
   - Harriet Tubman and the Underground Railroad
   - the Abolitionist movement in the United States

5. Research another instance of the oppression of a group of people. Present your findings in an oral or written report to your class. Some possibilities include
   - U.S. government policy toward Native Americans
   - apartheid in South Africa
   - Armenian massacre (1915–1922)
   - Holocaust (1930s and 1940s)
   - internment of Japanese Americans during World War II
   - the mass killing of Cambodians (1975–1979)
   - Iraqi attempts to exterminate the Kurdish minority (1980s)
   - "ethnic cleansing" of Muslims in Bosnia-Herzegovina (1990s)

6. Find out more about the psychological effects of slavery on the enslaved.

continued

7. With a partner, find out what it was like to be a young person in the United States in the 1830s and 1840s. Present your findings in an oral report or a bulletin board display. You might divide the topic into the following categories:
   - schooling
   - work
   - family life
   - games

8. Prepare a report on U.S. relations with Britain and Spain in the 1830s and 1840s. Include information about each country's attitudes toward the slave trade.

9. Find out about the contributions of African Americans to one of the following aspects of American culture:
   - music
   - agriculture
   - literature
   - science and technology

   Present your findings in a poster that can be displayed in the classroom.

10. Prepare a report on the "back to Africa" movement led by Marcus Garvey in the 1920s.

The Artist's Studio

1. Imagine you work for a Northern newspaper in the 1830s. Draw an editorial cartoon about the aspects of the slave trade in New Orleans.

2. Imagine that you have been asked to design a cover for a new edition of *The Slave Dancer*. Decide what image should be on the cover and draw it. Don't forget to include the title and the author's name.

3. Create portraits of four or five of the main characters in *The Slave Dancer*. Review the descriptions of them in the novel. Then prepare your portraits, trying to reflect each person's appearance and personality as described in the novel.

4. With other students in your class, prepare a mural depicting some of the important scenes from the novel. Try to capture the mood of each scene.

5. Find out about the art of one of the West African peoples who were brought to the Americas as slaves. Make a poster that represents some of the styles, motifs, or symbols of that culture.

6. Make an illustrated timeline that shows some of the most important events in the history of African Americans in the United States.

7. Design a memorial to the Africans who died as a result of the slave trade. Decide where the memorial should be located. If possible, make a model of the memorial.

The Writer's Workshop

1. Imagine you are a reporter for a New Orleans newspaper. You have heard rumors that a boy who disappeared several months ago has returned. Interview Jessie about his experiences and then write an article for your newspaper based on the interview. Remember that

continued

Jessie may not be willing to tell you everything that happened to him. Be sure to write an attention-getting headline.

2. Imagine you are Jessie and write a poem that expresses your feelings about music after being on *The Moonlight*.

3. Write several entries for Captain Cawthorne's log describing key events in the novel from his point of view.

4. Imagine a meeting between Jessie and Ras in the North. Write a new chapter or passage for the novel in which Jessie describes the meeting.

5. Imagine you are Jessie. Write a letter to the president of the United States explaining your feelings about slavery after being on *The Moonlight*. Propose a solution to the problem that you think would be fair to slaveholders as well as to enslaved African Americans.

6. Write a poem or journal entry that expresses your feelings after reading *The Slave Dancer*.

The Speaker's Platform

1. Write a script for a television docudrama about the slave trade. Interweave factual information with dramatic scenes. Cast your production and either videotape it or put on a live performance.

2. Those who worked to abolish slavery had different ideas about what should happen to those who were freed. Some thought they should be returned to Africa, some thought they should be given a separate homeland in the western United States, and some thought they should be integrated into American society. With other students, debate the pros and cons of each of these ideas.

3. With other students in the class, perform one of the dialogue sequences from *The Slave Dancer*. Try to act and speak the way you think your character would. Use narration for clues to how your character should act. You may wish to use costumes or props for your presentation. Two dialogues are suggested below.
   • Bottom of page 21 ("Step forward, boy . . . ") to page 24 ("Ah . . . you finish, Spark.")
   • Page 81 ("Wait!" Stout commanded. . . .) to page 82 ("They've all talked against me. . . .")

4. Imagine you are to appear on a local cable TV show called *Book Beat*. The goal of the show is to introduce viewers to new books. You are going to talk about *The Slave Dancer*. For your presentation, summarize the plot without giving away the end, choose one dramatic passage to read aloud, and tell what you like about the novel.

5. Imagine you are going to produce a movie based on *The Slave Dancer*. Write a script for one key scene. Cast the movie and have the cast act out the scene.

6. Imagine that *The Moonlight* did not sink but was captured by the American ship that pursued it. Captain Cawthorne is being tried for the illegal activity of transporting enslaved Africans. You are the prosecuting attorney. You have questioned Jessie Bollier and heard his side of the story. Present your summation to the jury. (A *summation* is a lawyer's final statement about the innocence or guilt of the accused. The summation is delivered to the jury before it leaves the courtroom to decide the case.)